FREEDOM'S CALLING!

WILL YOU ANSWER?

FREEDOM'S CALLING!

WILL YOU ANSWER?

Carol Polzin

Published exclusively by Lulu.com
on behalf of
The Matlin Press, LLC.

Published exclusively by Lulu.com on behalf of The Matlin Press, LLC.
Printed in the United States of America
Designed by Laura Berscheit
Cover photo Copyright © klikk/Fotolia.com
Carol Polzin's photograph by Dawn R. Anderson

Page 17: Quote from *Index of Dependence* © The Heritage Foundation. By permission of The Heritage Foundation. Page 21: Excerpt © The Tax Foundation. By permission of The Tax Foundation. Pages 24 - 25: Excerpt from *The Federal Workforce Continues to Grow Under Obama Budget* © The Heritage Foundation, February 22, 2011. By permission of The Heritage Foundation. Pages 34 -35: Quoted material © Creators.com. By permission of Michelle Malkin and Creators Syndicate, Inc. Pages 57: Excerpt from *The Anti-Conscious Mandate: An Assault on the Constitution* © The Heritage Foundation, February 17, 2012. By permission of The Heritage Foundation.

ISBN 978-1-105-86278-6 (paperback)
ISBN 978-1-105-86283-0 (eBook)
Cataloging-in-Publication data for this book is available from the Library of Congress.

Finally, this publication was created with the intent to provide competent and reliable information. Every effort has been made to verify and substantiate all claims made herein. The author and publisher specifically disclaim any liability incurred arising from the use or application of any claims, supporting information, or content contained in this publication.

AUTHOR'S NOTE

Dear Americans:

I am a grassroots American. I wrote *Freedom's Calling! Will You Answer?* because I can no longer sit back and watch the dismantling of the most magnificent nation on Earth. So I decided to speak up and speak out!

I wrote this book to give busy Americans some important political issues of the day to consider. I discuss, from an American grassroots point of view, the potential impact that these issues could have on the lives of Americans, possibly forever.

It is important that we take the time to become well-informed on the issues of the day; so that we can make an educated vote as to who we think can best lead America in the years ahead. As Americans, this is our decision. We have our magnificent power to vote. We must use it. We all must vote on Tuesday, November 6, 2012. Our country needs us!

-Carol Polzin

Contents

AUTHOR'S NOTE   *v*

INTRODUCTION   11

CHAPTER ONE

     Socialism, Disrespect and the Redistribution of
Wealth   13

CHAPTER TWO

     The American Economy and Dependence on the
Government   17

     The High Price of Gas   18

     The Keystone XL Pipeline   20

     The Unfairness of Fairness   21

     Washington's Wasteful Spending   23

     What Will the American Economy
Look Like in 2012 and Beyond?   26

CHAPTER THREE

     The Invalidation of the United States Congress
and the "Shredding" of the U.S. Constitution   29

CHAPTER FOUR

     President Obama and the Illegal Aliens   33

CHAPTER FIVE

     President Obama and Terrorism   39

CHAPTER SIX

The Mosque at Ground Zero   45

CHAPTER SEVEN

Team Obama-Holder and the Enforcement of
the Rule of Law   51

CHAPTER EIGHT

Americans Fear President Obama: The Audacity
of *Obamacare*   *55*

CHAPTER NINE

The Tea Party Movement   59

CHAPTER TEN

The Crisis and Control Factory - Owned and
Operated by the Obama Administration   63

CHAPTER ELEVEN

The Intruder   65

CHAPTER TWELVE

The Warnings of Two American Presidents   67
James Madison   67
Ronald Reagan   67

CHAPTER THIRTEEN

President Barack Obama and the Aftermath of
His Presidency   69

CHAPTER FOURTEEN

    Americans Must Use Their Magnificent Power
    to Vote!   71

CONCLUSION

    Speak up!   75

IT'S UP TO US NOW!

    Some Ways to Contribute Your Time and
    Talents   77

INTRODUCTION

Everyone will be called upon, at one time or another, to exhibit the unknown courage that exists deeply within their character. The upcoming 2012 Presidential Election will be one of those times. It is imperative now that we all wake up, wise up, stand up and speak up loudly against the damage that President Barack Obama has done to America. In our own way, by using the talents that God has given each one of us, we must no longer stand for his assault on the last fragile framework of freedom and democracy that has managed to remain intact. Otherwise, if Barack Obama were re-elected in 2012, the magnificent achievements of the Founders, and those of America's courageous military men and women of today, would be reduced to insignificance and tossed into the dustbin of history forever.

On the surface, this election will be about the economy, *Obamacare,* unemployment, taxes, the price of gas, immigration, foreign policy, war and other issues which reflect the political differences between the Democrats and Republicans. However, in the end, the 2012 Presidential Election must be about coming to terms with how far off course we have wandered as a nation. We must reclaim the nobility that was once part of who we are as a free and benevolent people. Barack Obama must not be allowed to cause further damage to America. We are smarter than that. Americans must non-violently take a stand and not hold back. The stakes are too high. There is no room for indifference.

The following series of mini-essays discuss, from the perspective of a *"Grassroots"* American, some of the most controversial issues of the day. These issues could affect the possible downfall of American freedom. Your duty is to decide what your position is. Then vote! We must remember that it is an extraordinary honor and privilege to be an American and live in the greatest nation on Earth. Yet, we are on the verge of losing that privilege because of President Obama's deep-down-disrespect of American values that he makes little attempt to conceal. We can do it! We must stay informed. We must vote. This election could possibly be the most crucial election in American history.

CHAPTER ONE

Socialism, Disrespect and the Redistribution of Wealth

"Socialism is a philosophy of failure, the creed of ignorance, and the gospel of envy. Its inherent virtue is the equal sharing of misery."
-Winston Churchill

Upon first glance, it would seem that socialism and its supposed doctrine of fairness might be beneficial; however, a deeper analysis of socialism reveals that it ends up not being fair at all. Socialism encourages and rewards dependency and leads to the loss of individual liberty. President John Adams, wrote to fellow-Founder, President Thomas Jefferson, on February 2, 1816, that, *"Power always thinks it has a great soul and vast views, (that are) beyond the comprehension of the weak."* In many of his writings, President Adams wrote not only to his present circumstances, but he wrote also to posterity and to the generations of Americans to come. Now, nearly 200 years after President Adams penned this letter to Jefferson, America finds itself in a similar dilemma. This time, it is President Barack Obama who has underestimated the intelligence of the American people and their dedication to protecting American freedom.

"Fundamentally transforming" America into a third-rate socialist non-entity does not require any allegiance, on President Obama's part, to preserving and protecting America's exceptionalism. Where liberty and freedom reign, a society flourishes. The absence of government oppression encourages a society to use their myriad of talents and skills for the advancement of their personal well-being. They are then free to use these talents and skills toward making the vital contributions to America and to the world that have resulted

in, for example:

- The eradication of polio by the development of the Salk Polio Vaccine;
- America's extraordinary accomplishments in space;
- America's advancements in biomedical engineering, lifesaving medical instruments and techniques;
- America's contributions to cardiac care and surgery;
- America's leading-edge contributions to the computer industry, which virtually changed and enlightened the entire world forever.
- America's benevolent efforts to abolish hunger and poverty in the world.

Where liberty and freedom perish, there is only disrespect and indifference toward the special qualities, ideas and talents that each American has to offer. There is no *flourishing* in a socialist society; only *sameness* and untold, calculated dependence on the government. Why, then, has this been the cornerstone of President Obama's agenda?

It is unfortunate that he has awarded himself an artificial license to interfere with the lives of Americans. They could become so dominated by the power of his new, expanded government and so legally regimented by the same, that automatic compliance would be certain to follow. That is not America. It is clear that the dependence of the American people upon the U.S. Government is the name of the President's game. Manipulating our financial and banking markets; dictating what health care insurance we purchase; and taxing us into servitude are just the beginning of a long list of maneuvers the Obama Administration intends to use. They then attempt to redistribute its *wealth,* from the ones who earned it through hard work, determination, ingenuity and, many times, years of additional education, to the ones who did not do so.

However, most Americans agree that the concept of helping those who truly are in need of assistance has never been the issue. But, President Obama has used it as a way to further divide the American people. Rep. Paul Ryan (R-WI), Chairman of the House Budget Committee, challenged President Obama's attempts to instigate this example of class warfare among Americans, when he said, *"We (Americans) believe in upward mobility; we believe in economic opportunity and prosperity, helping people who haven't had a chance at success, get there; not demonizing the people who have already reached success in their lives."*

The most compelling questions we must now ask ourselves are:

- Are our lives any better, any more prosperous, any more productive, since Barack Obama was elected in 2008?
- How has his massive government over-spending, and the prospect of our personal financial ruin, been working for us?
- Have we checked our 401K's lately?
- Do we even have a job anymore?
- What type of future will our children and grandchildren have if we are taxed and regulated to the point of dependence on the government?
- How have the government bailouts of the banks and the auto industry stimulated the economy?
- How has increased government regulation on businesses created jobs and helped the U.S. unemployment rate?

Whatever happens, the most difficult-to-fathom-aspect of President Obama's actions is that they have been intentional and deliberate by design. The downgrade of America's financial condition and the loss of respect for the United States worldwide have all been carefully planned and carried out by the Obama Administration. So far, the American people are close to being the losers. Yet, attempts by President Obama to destroy American capitalism, and the creative American entrepreneurial spirit that is its foundation, have not been entirely successful. We will see. We must stay aware.

CAROL POLZIN

Is this really freedom?

What do _you_ think?

CHAPTER TWO

The American Economy and Dependence on the Government

"Today, more people than ever before – 67.3 million Americans, from college students to retirees to welfare beneficiaries – depend on the federal government for housing, food, income, student aid, or other assistance once considered to be the responsibility of individuals, families, neighborhoods, churches, and other civil society institutions."

-Bill Beach
2012 Index of Dependence on Government
The Heritage Foundation

While he now professes to want to reduce the size of the national debt, President Obama has continued to increase it by $1 trillion a year to a whopping $15.6 trillion as of May, 2012. He has managed to raise the American debt to a point where the country is on the edge of bankruptcy. Now he proclaims that we need to get it under control and reduce it. Even so, the debt keeps rising, and he does not seem to have a plan in the works to reduce it. So far, President Obama continues to respond to the overwhelming objections and outcries of the American people to reduce the national debt and cut government spending with inaction and meaningless rhetoric.

Is President Obama worried about the well-being and prosperity of the American people? Not a chance. His only concern seems to be his re-election in 2012. If he has to manipulate his policies, such as they are, to be compatible with the political trend of the day or moment, he will do so. He appears to be incapable of understanding that Americans are not as clueless as he thinks they are. The American people are tired of being *jerked around* by the Obama Administration.

They are tired of being afraid of a government that dishonestly picks at and tampers with their lives, just because it can. The American people want jobs. They need leadership. They need peace of mind.

So what do we have to show for our almost $16 trillion? Not much.

- Our public school systems are in disarray.
- *Obamacare* has taken over one-sixth of the American economy.
- According to Senator John Thune (R-SD), *"The new health care laws (The Patient Protection and Affordable Act and the Health Care and Education Reconciliation Act of 2010), together known as the Affordable Care Act, come with an estimated price tag of $2.5 trillion over 10 years of full implementation (2014-2023), and these laws represent a restructuring of one-sixth of the American economy."*
- Millions of Americans have lost their homes due to foreclosure.
- 46.2 million Americans have had to resort to Food Stamps in 2012 (U.S. Department of Agriculture).
- $700 billion of U.S. taxpayers' money was wasted on President Obama's bailout of the auto industry and banks (TARP).
- Gasoline prices are at an unforgivable high and getting higher as of April, 2012.

The High Price of Gas

The real cause of the rising cost of a commodity is based on the law of supply and demand. This holds true for the rising prices that Americans are forced to pay at the gas pumps. Why is the Obama Administration increasing EPA (Environmental Protection Agency) regulations on the coal mining industry and the oil industry? Would it be that its goal is to over-regulate these industries to the point of extinction? That is not what this president was elected to do. President Obama was elected to do his job. He was elected to represent all of the American people by positively pushing for those programs and policies which best serve to stimulate the life of the American economy and advance it to a level that reflects the collective input and talents of all Americans.

It is not the government's job to reduce the price of gasoline. Rather, it is the government's job to help create a healthy business environment in which the oil industry (or any industry, for that matter) can thrive. Lower pricing would eventually result. But this cannot happen under President Obama's present energy program. Unless the Obama Administration stops pounding the American oil industry with regulations and stops trying to take control of it, (just as they did with American health care), the price of gas will continue to rise to an unmanageable level. Why then does President Obama steadfastly refuse to consider drilling for America's own oil and natural gas resources? Could it be that taking control of another major portion of the American economy (Energy) is another step in President Obama's plan to promote Americans' dependence on the government and, this time, on foreign oil resources? Will America's competitive edge in the global economic markets be sharpened or dulled by the government's overtaking the U.S. Energy industries? Does this fit the pattern of President Obama's socialism/dependence agenda?

By not releasing the stifling rules and regulations he has imposed upon oil companies, President Obama's goal continues to be the expansion and power and control of the U.S. government. It is like the domino effect:
- When Americans pay higher gasoline prices,
- They can't purchase as many products and services;
- This further squeezes our struggling economy;
- Companies' margins and profitability then decline;
- Thus negatively affecting the prospects for more jobs creation.

CAROL POLZIN

The Keystone XL Pipeline

When our Canadian friends asked the United States to participate in the construction of the new Keystone XL Pipeline, many Americans, with the exception of the President, saw it as an opportunity for more new jobs and a shot at a more lively economic growth. The Pipeline would have transported synthetic crude oil from the Athabasca Oil Sands in northeastern Alberta, Canada to destinations in the United States. Its proposed 1,700-mile route would include refineries in Illinois, the Cushing oil distribution hub in Oklahoma, and some proposed connections to refineries along the Gulf Coast of Texas.

While catering to the demands of his *progressive green* base, and never once deviating from his re-election campaign, President Obama has ignored the needs of Americans through intentional neglect and political design. At a January 18, 2012, press briefing in Washington, DC, a frustrated John Boehner, (R-OH) Speaker of the House, said, in response to the President's rejection of the Keystone XL Pipeline, *"There's really no way to put it. The President is selling out American jobs for politics."* By personally lobbying the Congress to disapprove the Pipeline, President Obama has forced Canada to look to China as a possible partner in this endeavor. The potential for new U.S. job opportunities and the hundreds of millions of dollars of new revenue that would have been generated by the Keystone Pipeline have been taken from our skilled American workers and shipped off to a foreign country that consistently rips off an inept, morally-challenged Obama Administration every chance they get.

Whenever there is an opportunity for Americans to regroup economically, it is the President who steps in and tries to shove his *green* energy and high gas prices down the throats of American citizens. Is his goal to wean Americans off of oil and petroleum forever and onto *green* energy alternatives? If so, *green* energy is not a practical solution for the lives of Americans at this time. Green energy is definitely worth pursuing for the future; however, its practical applications for our current needs are limited. Why is the Obama Administration using hundreds of millions of taxpayer dollars to support guaranteed loans to green energy companies? In 2009, for example, *Solyndra*, the failed solar panel company located in Fremont, CA, received $535 million in federal loan guarantees from the Obama Administration and then went out of business shortly thereafter. What happened to all of that taxpayer money? Where did it go?

The Unfairness of Fairness

All of this is being carried out by the Obama Administration in the name of social and financial *fairness*. Is it fair to discourage individual initiative and creativity? Is it fair that Americans are forced to pass on the results of their many achievements and accomplishments to the masses? Is it fair when:

- *The top 1% of U.S. taxpayers pay 36.4% of the income taxes in the U.S.?*
- *The top 10% of U.S. taxpayers pay 70% of the income taxes in the U.S.?*
- *Of the remaining percentage, 50% pay zero income taxes at all?*

-*The Tax Foundation*
Washington, DC
Note: The Tax Foundation is a non-partisan research organization that has monitored fiscal policy at the federal, state and local levels since 1937.

The majority of Americans recognize that there will always be situations where individuals will fall upon hard times and need the assistance of their fellow Americans. Americans are a compassionate people, who understand that there can be serious bumps along the road in every person's life. However, it is the intentional abuse of federal and state programs and funds, by people who can, but are unwilling to take responsibility for their own lives, that is the basis for the economic dilemma at hand. Is this really fair?

The following is a short story wherein a conservative father and his college student daughter talk about the unfairness of fairness.

Father & Daughter Talk
-Author Unknown

A young woman was about to finish her first year of college. Like so many others her age, she considered herself to be very liberal, and among other liberal ideals, she was very much in favor of higher taxes to support more government programs; in other words, redistribution of wealth.

She was deeply ashamed that her father was a rather staunch conservative, a feeling she openly expressed. Based on the lectures that she had participated in, and the occasional chat with a professor, she felt that her father had for years harbored an evil, selfish desire to keep what he thought should be his.

One day she was challenging her father on his opposition to higher taxes on the rich and the need for more government programs. The self-professed objectivity proclaimed by her professors had to be the truth, and she indicated so to her father. He responded by asking how she was doing in school.

Taken aback, she answered rather haughtily that she had a 4.0 GPA, and let him know that it was tough to maintain; insisting that she was taking a very difficult course load and was constantly studying, which left her no time to go out and party like other people she knew. She didn't even have time for a boyfriend, and didn't really have many college friends because she spent all her time studying.

Her father listened and then asked, "How is your friend Audrey doing?" She replied, "Audrey is barely getting by. All she takes are easy classes. She never studies, and she barely has a 2.0 GPA. She is so popular on campus; college for her is a blast. She's always invited to all the parties, and lots of times she doesn't even show up for classes because she's too hung over."

Her wise father asked his daughter, "Why don't you go to the Dean's Office and ask him to deduct 1.0 off your GPA and give it to your friend, who only has a 2.0? That way, you will both have a 3.0 GPA. Certainly that would be a fair and equal distribution of GPA."

The daughter, visibly shocked by her father's suggestion, angrily fired back, "That's a crazy idea. How would that be fair? I've worked really hard for my grades! I've invested a lot of time, and a lot of hard work! Audrey has done next to nothing toward her degree. She played while I worked my tail off!"

The father slowly smiled, winked and said gently, "Welcome to the conservative side of the fence." End of conversation.

Washington's Wasteful Spending

"Washington should focus on re-igniting the unmatched power of the American entrepreneurial spirit by sweeping away government red tape, expanding markets for U.S. goods, making it easier for small businesses to compete in the global market, and reducing our national debt by eliminating wasteful Washington spending."
-Senator John McCain (R-AZ)

Washington's wasteful spending continues to hamper a healthy American economic recovery and the reduction of our national debt. Washington has proclaimed that Americans must cut back their spending and tighten their belts. Yet, they persist in their reckless ways with little concern for the damaging effects they will have on the American economy and the lives of American citizens.

The Government Accountability Office (GAO) recently released their report entitled, *2012 Annual Report: Opportunities to Reduce Duplication, Overlap and Fragmentation.* To summarize, they reported that the U.S. Government is wasting *tens of billions of dollars* each year in duplication and overlap of already-existing programs. While testifying in a February 28, 2012, hearing before the House Oversight and Government Relations Committee, Mr. Gene Dodrano, Comptroller General for the U.S., said, *"Collectively, these reports show that, if the actions (to reduce the duplication and overlapping) are implemented, the government could potentially save tens of billions of dollars annually."*

All the while, the Obama Administration continues to expand the size of government bureaucracy, and looks the other way when it comes to the damaging effects brought on by its wasteful spending habits. The expansion of the government workforce has been one way for the Obama Administration to step up their assault on the private business sector of the economy. As stated in the article by the Heritage Foundation below, when all is said and done, *"The problem with all these additional government jobs is that government spending does not create the economic growth needed to sustain private sector job growth."* The article continued:

- *"Since the beginning of the last recession (December 2007) to February 2011, the private sector workforce has shrunk by 6.6%, while shedding more than 7.5 million jobs.*
- *Over that same period of time, the Federal Government workforce (excluding Census and Postal Workers) has grown by 11.7%, while adding 230,000 jobs.*
- *Since President Barack Obama was sworn into office, the private sector workforce has shrunk by 2.6%,*

while shedding 2.9 million jobs. The federal workforce (excluding Census and Postal Workers) has grown by 7%, while adding more than 144,000 jobs.

- *President Obama's FY 2012 budget proposes adding even more people to the federal payroll. The President wants to create an additional 15,000 Federal Government jobs, including 4,182 additional Internal Revenue Service employees; 1,054 of which will be needed to implement Obamacare alone."*

-The Federal Workforce Continues
to Grow Under Obama Budget
By Conn Carroll
The Heritage Foundation – February 22, 2011

It is difficult to comprehend the nature of The Obama Administration's disregard for the economic stability of America. Below is a sampling of some of the most outrageous Federal grants that were awarded by President Obama's Economic Stimulus Package, and the costs paid for them by the U.S. taxpayers. It is inexcusable and insulting that these grants, totaling over $60 million, have been awarded to superfluous projects in a time when many Americans are struggling to buy groceries. Where is the justification for our silence?

Some Federal grants that were awarded by the Economic Stimulus Bill:

$500,000.
To Study the Genetic Makeup of Ants...
Half a million dollars went to Arizona State University to study the genetic makeup of ants to determine distinctive roles in ant colonies.

$3.4 Million.
To build an *"ecopassage"* to help turtles cross a highway in Tallahassee, FL.

$325,000.
To Study the Mating Decisions of Female Cactus Bugs...

For the University of Florida to determine how the environment affects the mating decisions of the females Cactus Bugs.
$210,000.
To Study the Learning Patterns of Honeybees by the University of Hawaii.
$15,551.
To Study Drunk Mice...
The Rodent Study at Florida Atlantic University in Boca Raton, used $15,551, to pay for two summer researchers to help gauge how alcohol affects a mouse's motor function.
$2 Million.
To Extend and Restore *"The Crookedest Railroad in the World"*...
A $2 million grant went to extend an antique tourist line, the Virginia & Truckee Railway, built during Nevada's silver mining boom. The line currently ends near Mound House, home to several legal brothels, including the Kit Kat Guest Ranch and the Moonlight Bunny Ranch, but would go to Carson City.
$54 Million.
For the Napa Valley Wine Train...
$54 million stimulus dollars to build a new rail bridge, to elevate and relocate 3,300 ft. of tracks and to put flood walls around the train's station.

Total Cost to U.S. Taxpayers: $60,450,551.

-Compiled by the analysts at
The Senate Republican Communication Center
Washington, DC

What Will the American Economy Look Like in 2012 and Beyond?

It is clear that success and prosperity have not had a place in the Obama Administration's plan for the American economy. The power and massive expansion of the Federal Government is the cornerstone of the present administration, and it has not fostered the economic growth that is so badly needed in America. Businesses and industries keep taking one step forward and two steps back. As individual Americans, we feel it is not our fault. But, it will be, if we do not take action and vote in November. For now, the outlook for the American economy does not look inviting. President Obama continues to refuse to open up the markets to more competition, through lower taxes and less regulations. If he did, businesses would have more incentive to expand their brands more widely. Instead, they are forced to wait on the sidelines, with hundreds of millions of dollars of cash in hand, until things on the economic horizon look less tenuous and much more promising.

According to a report released by the Congressional Budget Office (CBO)*, on January 31, 2012, that American economic horizon looks like this:

- *"CBO projects 2012 GDP (Gross Domestic Product)** to increase just 2%.*
- *Growth will slow to just 1.1% in 2013 because of tax increases, spending cuts, and other factors.*
- *Unemployment rate will remain above 8% both this year (2012) and next (2013).*
- *U.S. deficit will be $1.1 trillion in 2012, the fourth consecutive year above $1 trillion.*
- *The Social Security Disability Insurance trust fund will be exhausted in 2016.*
- *Under current law, the debt will grow $3.1 trillion over the next 10 years.*
- *The Medicare hospital insurance trust fund will be exhausted in 2022."*

-The Congressional Budget Office Report
January 31, 2012

*Note: The Congressional Budget Office is a non-partisan Federal agency within the Legislative Branch of the U.S. Government that provides economic data analysis to the Congress. —Wikipedia
**Note: The GDP is the market value of all final goods and services produced within a country in a given year. —Wikipedia

What will the economic horizon of future generations of Americans look like? Will they be able to grow up in a society that recognizes them for their talent and the remarkable contributions to society that they can make? It is the duty of every American, to pass on to their children and grandchildren, a legacy where they are free to explore and discover their potential. A huge European, one-size fits all American economy, based on the people's dependence on the government, will only serve to destroy the exceptional American entrepreneurial spirit and ensure a future of debt and obligation for the innocent generations of Americans to come.

Is this really freedom?

What do _you_ think?

CHAPTER THREE

The Invalidation of the United States Congress and the "Shredding" of the U.S. Constitution

"No man is good enough to govern another without the other's consent."

-Abraham Lincoln

With all of the power and majority support that were laid at his feet when he first took office, President Obama had unrestricted and boundless opportunity to strengthen and improve the lives of all Americans and to trumpet the majesty of peace and freedom around the world. Instead, he turned on America and chose to disrespect and to circumvent the U.S. Congress and the U.S. Constitution. Given more time and if re-elected in 2012, President Obama could continue his in-your-face efforts to invalidate the prestige and influence of the Congress.

President Obama and his administration are working toward rendering the Congress irrelevant. This could eventually reduce the Congress to nothing more than a benign, rubber stamp, ineffective government entity. When President Obama cannot secure congressional passage of a bill, he uses *When-All-Congressional-Means-Fail-Invoke-Executive-Orders.* One example of this is his 2009 Executive Order to close *Gitmo* in Cuba. Another example is his Executive Order to stop the automatic deportation of illegal aliens, even though the Dream Act was defeated in 2010. Let it be known that President Obama uses his power of executive orders when he does not get his own way. He overrides the Congress without regard for the will of the American people.

CAROL POLZIN

Barack Obama has shown his true colors. For nearly four years, Americans have experienced deceit, theatrics and the secret manipulation and arrogant disregard of the American rule of law by the Obama Administration. We now see what we have suspected almost from the beginning. The dark and murky colors that are the hues of tyranny daily keep rising to the surface of a President who lacks the moral character and conviction to lead America with honor and integrity. Instead, America is being destroyed right before our eyes – right in front of us. Who would do such a thing? Who would want to go down in history forever as the President who intentionally destroyed the free American way of life? Who would want to be remembered in history for such a deplorable act? What then are President Obama's real goals?

Does he want to impose as many tyrannical Executive Orders upon Americans as possible before the November election? Is he trying to wield as much power as he can in a last-minute crash and burn effort to destroy American freedom and shred the Constitution? His efforts to invalidate the U.S. Congress have reached the point now where he simply circumvents them. He then moves on to foreign global panels (like NATO and the United Nations) to further humiliate Americans by apologizing to these international entities for America; then asking for their permission to go to war in Libya and possibly war in Syria in the near future.

Perhaps the most stunning, revealing example of the Obama Administration's intentions took place during a March 7, 2012, hearing of the Senate Armed Services Committee in Washington, DC. During the hearing, U.S. Defense Secretary, Leon Panetta, informed the Committee that he would seek *"international permission,"* rather than Congressional approval, before taking military action in Syria.

The following is an excerpt from the discussion between Committee member, Senator Jeff Sessions (R-AL), and Secretary Panetta:

Senator Sessions: *"Do you think you can act without Congress and initiate a no-fly zone in Syria without congressional approval?"*
Secretary Panetta: *"Our goal would be to seek international permission...Whether or not we would want to get permission from the Congress – I think those are issues we would have to discuss as we decide what to do here."*
Senator Sessions: *"Well, I am almost breathless about that because what I heard you say is, 'We're going to seek international approval and we'll come and tell the Congress what we might do, and we might seek congressional approval.' ---Wouldn't you agree that would be pretty breathtaking to the average American?"*

This would mean that if the United States found it necessary to go to war, they would need to get the permission of the United Nations Security Council, of which China and Russia are permanent *card-carrying* members. This is truly a warning of major proportions to all Americans. Our safety and security are being dangerously compromised by a President who is contemptuous of the Congress and snubs and degrades the Constitution. Unfortunately for the American people, this President is willing to sacrifice American liberty and security for world power and control. Mr. Panetta's testimony is an example of what the Obama Administration has in store for America. Think what could happen to our lives if President Obama were re-elected for another four years. Chances are that the American way of life, which is based on individual freedom and watched over by the Constitution, would meet a painful and agonizing demise at the hands of abrasive radical liberals and their chief, Barack Obama.

President Obama had it all with his enormous base of power, his beautiful family and his charming charisma. However, there is one important part of him that has always mysteriously been missing. A deep-down-in-your-gut-patriotic-love of America is nowhere to be found in his rhetoric, his policies and his commitment, as President of the United States, to promoting simple decency as the core foundation of our once wise and noble nation. Is it possible that he doesn't realize that the socialist society for which he yearns, is not possible where freedom and democracy exist? Or maybe he does, and he is doing something about it.

Is this really freedom?

What do _you_ think?

CHAPTER FOUR

President Obama and the Illegal Aliens

"Fathom the hypocrisy of a government that requires every citizen to prove he is insured but not everyone must prove he is a citizen."
-Author Unknown

Here is Barack Hussein Obama, President of the United States of America; a former professor of Constitutional Law; supposedly a graduate of Harvard Law School; captain of all the Far Left radicals in this country. Still, he must resort to underhanded/unconstitutional means, rather than intellect and merit, to ram his legislation through the Congress. If President Obama, for example, were secure in his agenda and confident in the support of the American people, his re-election would not cause him undue concern. He would not be pressed then to court the American Latino vote by proposing amnesty for illegal aliens.

It is an insult to all law-abiding American citizens and legal residents, who have honorably worked within the legal framework of America their entire lives, to watch President Obama propose to reward those who are in the United States illegally with an easier road to American citizenship status. It does not take much intellectual prowess to convert someone, with little funding or means, to the ways of a determined, cunning socialist; a socialist who will sue any state government that tries to legally protect its own citizens from murder, drug cartels and the creepy slithering of terrorists under and over America's intentionally-unsecured-and-dangerous-borders.

As if President Obama's cavalier disregard for the security of America weren't enough, in May 2010, he brought Mexican President, Felipe Calderon, into the center of all American democracy. There he allowed President Calderon to lecture a

Joint Session of the United States Congress on his contempt
for Arizona's newly-passed immigration law and how illegal
immigrants are treated in the United States. President Calderon
conveniently forgot to mention, in his speech to the Congress,
however, just how illegal immigrants are treated in <u>his</u> country.
Here is a sampling taken from an April 28, 2010, article written
for *Creators Syndicate* by Michelle Malkin (an American author,
conservative blogger and political commentator) entitled, *How
Mexico Treats Illegal Aliens:*

- *"The Mexican Government will bar foreigners if they upset
  <u>the equilibrium of the national demographics</u>. How's that
  for racial and ethnic profiling?*
- *If outsiders do not enhance the country's <u>economic or
  national interests</u> or are <u>not found to be physically or
  mentally healthy</u>, they are not welcome. They must not be
  economic burdens on (Mexican) society or security.*
- *Those seeking Mexican citizenship must show a birth
  certificate, <u>provide a bank statement proving economic
  independence</u>, pass an exam and <u>prove that they can
  provide their own health care.</u>*
- *Illegal entry into Mexico is equivalent to a felony
  punishable by two years' imprisonment.*
- *Document fraud and marriage fraud are subject to a fine
  and imprisonment.*
- *Evading deportation is a serious crime; illegal re-entry
  after deportation is punishable by ten years' imprisonment.*
- *Foreigners may be kicked out of Mexico <u>without due
  process.</u>*
- *Law enforcement officials at all levels – by national
  mandate – must cooperate to enforce Mexican immigration
  laws, including illegal alien arrests and deportations.*
- *Native-born Mexicans are empowered to make citizens'
  arrests of illegal aliens and turn them in to authorities.*
- *Ready to show your papers? Mexico's National Catalog of
  Foreigners tracks all outside tourists and foreign nationals.*

A National Population Registry tracks and verifies the identity of every member of the population, who must carry a citizens' identity card. Visitors who do not possess proper documents and identification are subject to arrest as illegal aliens."

-By permission of Michelle Malkin and
Creators Syndicate, Inc.

President Obama's unconstitutional refusal to *"protect each state from invasion"* (Article 4, Section 4, U.S. Constitution) has already resulted in the tragic death of a highly-respected young AZ border patrol officer, Brian Terry (December 14, 2010). Mr. Terry was shot and killed, by a Mexican criminal. He was shot with one of the 2,000 guns that the U.S. Department of Justice intentionally allowed to cross the border into Mexico as a part of their failed Fast and Furious gun-walking scheme. Then there was the senseless murder, by an illegal alien, of an Arizona rancher, Robert Krentz, <u>on his own property</u>, on March 27, 2010. Equally appalling was the murder of New Mexico rancher, Larry Link, (June 6, 2011), who had responded to information that there was possibly an illegal alien on his property. Both ranchers were widely known for going out of their way to help anyone who was in need. How long is President Obama going to ignore the tragedy that his failure to secure America's borders has cost, in terms of the innocent lives that have been lost and the damage to property that has resulted?

Further, in July of 2011, The Treasury Inspector General for Tax Administration (TIGTA), (an office established in 1998 to provide independent oversight of IRS activities), reported that the government payout on the tax credit to illegal aliens more than quadrupled from **$924 million** in 2005 to a **staggering $4.2 billion** paid by U.S. taxpayers in 2010. The TIGTA stated that, *"An increasing number of individuals (illegal aliens) are filing tax returns claiming the Additional Child Tax Credit*

(ACTC), a refundable tax credit intended for working families. The payment of Federal funds through this tax benefit appears to provide an additional incentive for aliens to enter, reside and work in the United States without authorization." The TIGTA's audit also found that 72% of the tax returns filed in 2010 claimed this refundable Additional Child Tax Credit.

Senator Orrin Hatch (R-Utah), ranking member of the Senate Finance Committee, stated on September 2, 2011, that, *"the disconcerting findings in this report demand immediate attention and action from Congress and the Obama Administration. With our debt standing at over $14.5 trillion and counting, it's outrageous that the IRS is handing out tax credits to those who aren't even eligible to work in this country."*

The problem of illegal immigration will not go away until Americans elect a President and a Congress who have the courage to face this bold-faced example of corruption. Only when America's dangerous borders are finally secured, will President Obama's assault on our safety come to a conclusion. Until companies who hire illegal aliens are sanctioned and the easy road to American citizenship no longer exists, the problem of illegal immigration will continue unobstructed. Until free college tuition for children of illegal aliens is no longer an option, and illegal aliens no longer receive the free health care that U.S. taxpayers provide, they will continue to seek the blissful harbor that was created by the hard work of the citizens and legal residents of the United States.

It is important to remember, however, that America has always welcomed those immigrants who come to this country legally, bringing with them their special skills and talents to share. They must be recognized and appreciated for their efforts to legally enter the United States. They stood in line like everyone else and dutifully completed the required paperwork and followed the myriad of procedures to finally enter the United States the legal way. They are the immigrants who respect the American rule of law and, by example, teach their children to do the same. They become active and valued members of the American society, and cherish all of the opportunities that exist in America for them to build a healthy and prosperous life for themselves and their families. That is legal immigration, and it is welcomed.

So, an agenda of pride and accomplishment on which President Obama can then base a re-election bid is a challenge to find when you consider:

- an inexcusable 8.2% U.S. unemployment rate *(Bureau of Labor Statistics, March 2102)*;
- a massive $15.6 trillion-and-climbing-national debt *(U.S. National Debt Clock, April 2012)*;
- his unconstitutional refusal *"to protect each state from Invasion"* (Article 4, Section 4, U.S. Constitution);
- the intentional destruction of America's world premier health care system in the name of socialism; and
- his arrogant neglect of his duties as the world's chief steward of peace and freedom as part of his political resume for re-election.

What remains for President Obama is to again manipulate and twist the U.S. political system and the U.S. Constitution to his glorification; thereby cheapening the very ideals of freedom and democracy to which he attaches his name. Even if he were re-elected, how can Americans trust the sincerity of his dainty pirouetting to the center? Then once taking office, what is there to stop him from returning to his cozy political home on the left?

Is this really freedom?

What do _you_ think?

CAROL POLZIN

CHAPTER FIVE

President Obama and Terrorism

"This is not a battle between the United States of America and terrorism, but between the free and democratic world and terrorism."

-*The Honorable Tony Blair*
Prime Minister of the United Kingdom,
1997-2007

Has Muslim Extremism, and the Jihad hatred and violence that it spews, been replaced by President Obama's political correctness policy as the new enemy of the United States? Where he is without resolve to protect America, President Obama tries to neutralize national security threats by wiping the slate clean through political correctness. Or worse, he ignores them, as he did during the Wikileaks espionage theft of crucial top secret portions of the intelligence and security of the United States. Where in the world was his outrage? It seems that political correctness and President Obama's indifference toward protecting Americans have become America's new enemies, to the extent that now the terrorists don't even have to pay the band to dance to the music.

So what must happen to the morale of our brave fighting men and women, the ones who have lost arms, legs and worse while defending this country? What must have it been like for them when they heard, for example, that their Commander in Chief wanted to bring the terrorists, who are currently being held at the U.S. military prison in Guantanamo Bay, Cuba (*Gitmo*), to New York City for trial in our U.S. civilian courts system? They would then be tried just a short distance from Ground Zero. Unfortunately, the first such Obama-Holder terror trial of this kind was held in New York City in November, 2010. As reported by the *New York Times,* on November 17, 2010, this first civilian/terror court trial resulted in a guilty verdict on one lone count of *conspiracy to destroy buildings of the United States by means of an explosive.* Worse yet, was the unthinkable acquittal on 284 other more serious counts of murder and terror for Ahmed Khalafan Ghailani, a former Guantanamo Bay (Cuba) terror detainee. The *New York Times* further reported that Ghailani was actually acquitted on four counts of conspiracy. These four counts included conspiring to kill Americans and conspiring to use weapons of mass destruction!

Ghailani was allegedly responsible for the bombings of the U.S. embassies in Africa and in Tanzania on August 7, 1998, and the subsequent mass murder of 224 innocent people. Although he was eventually sentenced to life in prison, Ghailani's acquittal, by an American court, on the 284 other more serious terror charges will remain a permanent, humiliating example of President Obama's *progressive* intentions to persistently fix what isn't broken. He always thinks he knows better. When will the Obama Administration do something of substance to reinforce and upgrade America's national security? This should not be happening in the United States of America.

Because of this travesty, the Congress, in the Lame Duck Session of 2010, wisely voted to forbid allocating funds for the transfer of enemy combatants from *Gitmo* to the United States for civilian trial; thus, forcing President Obama, in March, 2011, to rescind his original January, 2009 Executive Order. This Executive Order originally banned bringing any new charges against terror suspects in the military commissions. President Obama's and U.S. Attorney General, Eric Holder's, preposterous efforts to try the terrorists in American civilian courts and to close *Gitmo* would then be blocked. The use of military tribunals for terror trials would then be rightfully reinstated. It remains to be seen, however, if President Obama will choose to use other sources of funding and means to again ignore the will of the Congress and bring the terrorists to America for trial, anyway. He needs to work diligently every day to nourish the fragile state of peace; instead of diligently pretending every day that we are not at war.

By not taking every precaution to protect Americans, President Obama has recklessly exposed America to the vulnerability of more attacks. The terrorists have, for quite some time, enjoyed being coddled by him. So why would they fear any retribution from America now? It is no wonder that their attacks on America have increased. President Obama's continued indifference to his duties to protect America have frighteningly resulted in the Christmas Day, 2009, thwarted attempt to blow up a UK-to-Detroit-bound-airliner by a young Nigerian terrorist, known as, *The Underwear Bomber*. At his trial in Detroit, MI, on October 12, 2011, he pleaded *guilty* and later received the mandatory sentence of life in prison.

Tragically, there is a longer list of domestic terror attacks that took place on President Obama's watch – or lack thereof. One of them being the *Fort Hood (TX) Massacre,* when thirteen innocent people were killed, and dozens more wounded (November, 2009), by a radical Muslim militant, who happened to be a U.S. military officer of our own. As of 2012, he has yet to be tried. During a joint session of the Senate and House Homeland Security Committee (December, 2011), Senator Susan Collins (R-Maine) cited a letter from the U.S. Defense Department, in which they categorized the Fort Hood TX shootings as being due to *workplace violence*; rather than what it actually was, radical Islam. The absurdity of President Obama's political correctness policy and the threat to American national security that it continues to promote, serve to illustrate the danger in which the President of the United States of America has intentionally placed his own country.

Then, following the tragic events at Fort Hood, there were the botched car bombing attempt in Times Square, NY (May, 2010) and the wicked foiled Al Qaeda global mail bomb terror attack (October, 2010). Until President Obama takes seriously his constitutional duty to protect America, it is just a matter of time before Americans will again be the victims of his indifference.

His indifference continues. Reuters News Agency reported (December 29, 2011) that the Obama Administration's *secret* attempts at peace talks with the Taliban have resulted in the possibility that the Obama Administration might cave in to the Afghan High Peace Council's numerous requests for the release of the top five Taliban commanders. They are the hardened criminals and terrorists, who are currently being held at *Gitmo* in Cuba. Even if the five Taliban commanders are not released by President Obama, this serves to illustrate the dangerous, casual disregard in which he holds the security and safety of the United States. It is then compounded by his strange, misguided willingness to appease those who wish to kill us all. That President Obama would even consider acquiescing to the demands of the terrorists by releasing these Taliban murderers, is a slap in the face to all our military men and women who have fought and who still fight so valiantly to protect America from the far-reaching, violent tentacles of terrorism. His conciliatory attitude is a gross insult to the memory of the 3,000 innocent people who were killed by Islamic terrorists on September 11, 2001(9/11).

What motivates a man like Barack Obama to deliberately put us all in danger? Is he motivated by how he thinks history will treat him? Possibly. Or, is he motivated by contempt for America that comes from some hidden morally-corrupt agenda of his that is gradually oozing now from the wounds inflicted on us by his presidency? Perhaps the vitriolic ranting of his good friend, Reverend Jeremiah Wright, deeply affected President Obama, when he sat in Wright's congregation for twenty years listening to him trash and smear America, the last country in the world where he is free to preach his vulgar ideologies. Some of the other radical company the President keeps include:

- Bill Ayres, the unrepentant domestic terrorist of the violent 1960's Weather Underground Organization;
- Van Jones, President Obama's radical former Green Jobs Czar;
- And those at ACORN, the corrupt and not-so-defunct community organizing arm of the Obama Administration.

Perhaps, these people and others, have drained the President of any allegiance he might have held for America and replaced it, in his mind, with the destructive formula of:

Socialism
+A massive dose of government interference
+A boatload of arrogance
The loss of our freedom as we know it today.

Is this really freedom?

What do _you_ think?

CAROL POLZIN

CHAPTER SIX

The Mosque at Ground Zero

"Against the insidious wiles of foreign influence, (I conjure you to believe me fellow citizens) the jealousy (vigilance) of a free people ought to be constantly awake, since history and experience prove that foreign influence is one of the most baneful foes of Republican Government."

-George Washington,
Farewell Address,
September 19, 1796

President Obama's ultimate affront to the dignity of those who were killed on 9/11 was that he did nothing to publicly suggest an alternate solution to the hyper-controversial problem of the construction of the Muslim mosque in New York City next to Ground Zero. By ignoring the opposition of outraged Americans, and by making sure to mention the Muslims' right to build the mosque, President Obama telegraphed to the world his endorsement of this symbol of terror and hate. Even though the Muslims had the right to build their mosque at Ground Zero, President Obama could have used this opportunity to try to bring together our frightened, sad and injured nation. Instead, he chose to bow to the controversial, insensitive actions of those who could have been a healing inspiration by compassionately building their mosque at another site, other than Ground Zero. Three thousand innocent people perished on 9/11, and their grieving friends and families do not need any more reminders of all that they lost on that terrible day in 2001.

Pope John Paul II stood with compassion and integrity in 1993, when he called upon 14 Carmelite Nuns to move their convent further away from the location of the German concentration camp, Auschwitz. He recognized the potential for additional hurt and pain that the sight of the convent could cause. He realized that a Catholic convent located so closely to where thousands of Jews were tortured and killed by the Nazis, could remind those who survived, of a time of unthinkable horror and loss (Foxman, 2010).*The sad but striking difference between the actions of these two very different and famous men was that Pope John Paul II led by compassion and grace; while President Obama did not care to lead, at all.

Note: Abraham Foxman is a Soviet-born American activist and Director of the Anti-Defamation League(ADL). He is known throughout the world as a leader in the fight against Anti-Semitism and hatred.

The mosque at Ground Zero, its Ground Floor Islamic Cultural Center completed on September 21, 2011, has become a national issue of sadness and loss. It is no longer a local New York City zoning issue, involving a couple of blocks of New York City real estate and the historical status of an old downtown building next to Ground Zero. How could any president of this great country, especially in a time of war, stand by and do nothing to help shield the embattled, innocent Americans, whom he supposedly serves, from this cruel reminder of their loss and pain?

President Obama had an opportunity to graciously manage the controversy of the construction of the Muslim mosque at Ground Zero. He could have stepped up and been a true inspiration to all Americans by quietly and presidentially suggesting another location in New York City for the mosque to be built. But his indifference, and probably the debt he owes to those who have funded and continue to fund his presidency, will never allow for the true leadership he should have shown. So Americans, and particularly New Yorkers, must now face the possibility of the future completion of the rest of the 13-story restoration project of the building at 51 Park Place, in New York City, NY. If it were not for the new beautifully-peaceful and serene *National September 11th Memorial,* located at Ground Zero, it would be difficult for those who lost so much on 9/11 to heal, with the mosque at Ground Zero looming nearby.

> $1.5 billion taxpayer dollars sent to
> The Muslim Brotherhood in Egypt
> by President Obama on March 22, 2012

But, wait a minute! $1.5 billion of American taxpayer money (money that America does not have) was given, by President Obama, (March 22, 2012) to The Muslim Brotherhood to aid their military efforts in Egypt. This terrorist group is connected to the very Islamic extremists, like Osama bin Laden and Khalid Sheikh Mohammed, who shattered 3,000 lives on 9/11 and shook the heart of America's freedom at its very soul. A Congressional provision had previously restricted military aid to Egypt stating that, *"unless the State Department certifies that Egypt is making progress on basic freedoms and human rights,"* the United States would withhold all aid. Secretary of State, Hillary Clinton, however, on March 22, 2012, told Congress that she will waive this provision on the grounds that it affects the national interests of the United States. What national interests? During a December, 2011 interview with a local news channel out of Colorado Springs, CO, President Obama made it clear that should the Congress not agree with his policies, he would by-pass them. He said then, referring to his administration, *"And where Congress is not willing to act, we're going to go ahead and do it for ourselves."* He did just that. How can America withstand another four years of a President whose vision for this country is one of disregard of the very rules and laws that are its foundation; coupled with his dangerous, undisguised preference for those who wish us harm? What must our friends in Israel think about all of this?

As America and the victims' families and friends struggle to deal with the trauma and grief of 9/11, the President of the United States sends funds to a terrorist group that continues to shout its hatred of America and promote its violent Sharia Law. Think how that $1.5 billion could help the struggling citizens of this country.

- What about the families and emergency responders of 9/11?
- What about advances in medical research?
- What about the millions of U.S. homes in foreclosure?
- What about our veterans to whom America owes leading-edge care, rehabilitation and job opportunities?
- What about returning America to its former prominence in space?
- What about America's starving small businesses?

$1.5 billion could go a long way towards helping to resuscitate an injured and fragmented America. Unfortunately, it will not happen under this President.

Is this really freedom?

What do *you* think?

FREEDOM'S CALLING! WILL YOU ANSWER?

CAROL POLZIN

CHAPTER SEVEN

Team Obama-Holder and the Enforcement of the Rule of Law

"We must reject the idea that every time a law's broken, society is guilty, rather than the lawbreaker. It is time to restore the American precept that each individual is accountable for his actions."
-Ronald Reagan

With the assistance of his U.S. Attorney General, Eric Holder, and Mr. Holder's staff of Assistant Attorneys General in the Department of Justice, it becomes easier for the President and the U.S. Department of Justice to disregard the American rule of law by bypassing the very units of law and justice that they swore to uphold and protect.

For example, in August of 2011, President Obama took matters into his own hands, and signed another one of his *When-All-Congressional-Means-Fail-Invoke-Executive-Orders*, this time to halt the automatic deportation of illegal aliens. This essentially resulted in the back-door passage of the already-defeated (in December, 2010) Dream Act. If enacted, the Dream Act, would have, in general, provided amnesty to illegal aliens. At that time, even with a Democratic White House, and a Democratic majority in both the House and Senate, President Obama was unable to secure its congressional passage. So politically courting the American Latino vote, President Obama signed this Executive Order.

According to House Judiciary Chairman, Lamar Smith (R-TX), *"This appears to some in Congress as the President by-passing Congress and effectively creating laws through imposing regulations."*
"The new order permits," continued Rep. Smith:
- *"....hundreds of thousands of illegals to be given work*

authorizations, allowing them to compete with Americans for jobs;

- *a presidential task force to decide who receives amnesty and who does not, creating even more bureaucracy in Washington;*
- *the reversal of a judge's decision to send a person back to their home country."*

Another example begs the question: Where is it written that the President of the United States has the authority to declare an existing Federal law constitutional or unconstitutional? The President can sign a bill or he can veto it, but it is exclusively the responsibility of the U.S. Federal courts system to render such constitutional rulings. *"Two weeks ago, (March 1, 2011) President Obama made an unprecedented decision to declare a Federal Law (DOMA - The Defense of Marriage Act) unconstitutional and thereby abdicate his responsibility to uphold and defend that law,"* stated Rep. Dan Burton (R-IN) in *The Hill's Congressional Blog*, on March 14, 2011. DOMA, a law signed by President Clinton in 1996, defines marriage as a legal union between one man and one woman. Equally bold was President Obama's order to Attorney General Holder to stop defending this law in U.S. courts. *"I am deeply concerned that the President simply declared a law to be unconstitutional and one that he will not defend or enforce,"* continued Rep. Burton. Who gave them the authority to not enforce the rule of law because a law does not conform to their particular political posture or help their political cause of the moment? It is clear that the Obama Administration will continue to play their dangerous games until American citizens, in the voting booths, start holding them accountable for their free-wheeling dance around their duties and responsibilities to the American people.

In a brazen performance, the President of the United States publicly challenged the U.S. Supreme Court on their authority to declare a law to be constitutional or unconstitutional. The question of the constitutionality of *Obamacare* had just reached the Supreme Court on March 26, 2012. For the next two days, oral arguments were presented by both sides. President Obama, perhaps suspecting that the Supreme Court might have taken a dim view of *Obamacare,* publicly lashed out at them for possibly acting as *judicial activists* and potentially rendering an *unprecedented* decision; neither of which was true *(ref. Marbury v. Madison 1803).* Now we have the President of the United States admonishing the U.S. Supreme Court for the entire world to see. It was especially concerning for Americans when the President *carried on* during an April 2, 2012, joint visit to the White House by Canadian Prime Minister, Stephen Harper, and Mexican President, Felipe Calderon. Did President Obama, a former professor of constitutional law, selectively neglect to mention the Defense of Marriage Act (DOMA)? After all, President Obama, all by himself, declared DOMA unconstitutional in 2011, and then ordered Eric Holder not to defend it in U.S. courts.

In addition, instead of enforcing the rule of law, Attorney General Holder, dropped the case against the New Black Panthers in Pennsylvania. They were clearly caught on tape, brandishing nightsticks, trying to intimidate voters at a Philadelphia polling place on Election Day in 2008. When asked during a March 1, 2011, hearing of the House Appropriations Sub-Committee in Washington, DC, why he decided not to prosecute the New Black Panthers, Mr. Holder, an African American, answered that focusing so much attention on the New Black Panthers, *"demeans my people."* What? Doesn't Mr. Holder recognize that all Americans are his people?

Perhaps, it is Mr. Holder who is demeaning, or at least, disappointing all Americans, by not using the prestigious education he received at one of the finest law schools in the country (Columbia Law School in New York City, NY). He could have shown all Americans how to work together to move our country forward to exciting heights of success and prosperity. He could have used his considerable knowledge and experience to guide every one of us away from racism and all of its ugly implications. Instead, Mr. Holder preferred to revert to the racially turbulent times of the 1960's. If the Attorney General of the United States, who is the chief law enforcement officer of this land, will not impartially enforce the American rule of law, then who will?

Is this really freedom?

What do _you_ think?

CHAPTER EIGHT

Americans Fear President Obama: The Audacity of *Obamacare*

"When the people fear their government, there is tyranny; when the government fears the people, there is liberty."
                                                            -Thomas Jefferson

If he were sincerely acting on behalf of all Americans and doing so with the U.S. Constitution in mind, there would be no need for President Obama to look over his shoulder and secretly govern by *gimmicks* behind closed doors. Well-thought-through programs and policies that result in differences of opinion are easily forgiven. That's America. Intentional injustice aimed at destroying the American way of life is neither easily forgiven nor forgotten.

Many Americans are now afraid of the Obama Administration, especially President Obama, and worry that the daily control of their lives will be taken over by clueless government bureaucrats with the experience and compassion of a gnat. There is plenty of room to legislatively accommodate those who need assistance. That has never been the issue. However, a common-sense approach to helping those who need the assistance and President Obama's making it possible to do so by encouraging a robust business climate would have no realistic place in his socialist thinking. It seems that in his mind, all Americans must be reduced to the same level of mediocrity.

Then, he could declare, *"There will now be sub-standard health care for all!"* President Obama's health care reform law and his yet unattained dream of the *public option,* have nothing to do with reforming and improving the finest health care system in the world. Rather, they have everything to do with government oppression and the massive expansion and growth of Federal power.

President Obama strives for that power by gradually and methodically removing the rung of choice from the founding platform of our freedom. To this end, the health care reform law is an outrageous insult to all Americans. It is a frightening preview of the tyranny that could come our way, as the result of this unprecedented power-grab by the Federal Government and by President Obama, in particular. He and his fellow-Democrats in the Congress, railroaded this 2,700-page piece of legislation through the Congress by using every underhanded, behind-closed-doors-maneuver possible to compensate for the votes in the Congress that they did not have to pass it. This new health care reform law, or *Obamacare*, placing one-sixth of the American economy under the control of the Federal Government, was passed in spite of the overwhelming objections of the American people.

"In a proposed rule from Secretary Kathleen Sebelius and the Department of Health and Human Services (HHS), the federal government is demanding insurance companies submit detailed health care information about their patients," stated Rep. Tim Huelskamp, (R-KS) (Washington Examiner, Op-Ed, September, 23, 2011.) Ms. Sebelius attempted to justify this proposal on the basis that the HHS needs the medical care information of every patient, in order to compare the job performance of each private health care insurance company. The real purpose of this proposed regulation, however, is for the HHS to begin building a database of the medical care records of all Americans. This highly-confidential information will be used by the government, in the very near future, to begin dictating whether or not a patient is eligible to receive, for example, that heart surgery, that hip replacement or the timely treatment of a life threatening disease.

It is all about power, money, control and disrespect - nothing more. This is just the beginning of the many hidden regulations in *Obamacare* that Americans will soon have to confront. It is disturbing to note that the confidentiality of our personal medical care records will soon be scrutinized by the medically-untrained likes of Kathleen Sebelius, President Obama and the government that passed *Obamacare* without regard for, and at the expense of, our individual rights and freedom.

Since its passage in 2009, *Obamacare* has been touted as a national program that will provide *free* health care for all Americans. Free? How so? *Obamacare* is a law that was passed by manipulation, bribery, and coercive means. It was not passed to provide free health care for all Americans. Instead, it was passed to further promote the intrusion into American lives of the U.S. Government. Why? Could it be about government power and control?

Of significant note, is *Obamacare's* assault on Americans' religious freedoms. *Obamacare,* contains what is called, The Anti-Conscience Mandate. Therein, it decrees that:

- *"All insurance plans must cover, at no charge, abortion-inducing drugs, contraceptives, sterilization and patient education and counseling for women of reproductive age.*
- *Religious employers, such as Catholic hospitals, Christian schools, and faith-based pregnancy care centers, will have to provide and pay for such coverage for their employees, regardless of their religious beliefs.*
- *In what some have called the narrowest religious exemption in federal law to date, only houses of worship are exempted.*
- *The Administration also published guidelines on February 10, 2012, giving one year for religious groups to "adapt" to the rule that runs counter to their religious beliefs.*
- *The moral compass for some of our most intimate life decisions is now in the hands of bureaucrats."*

-Obamacare Anti-Conscience Mandate:
An Assault on the Constitution
The Heritage Foundation - February 17, 2012

CAROL POLZIN

What exactly is it about *Obamacare* that is free?

Is it free when *Obamacare* will dictate to Americans which doctor they can see? Is it free when *Obamacare* mandates what X-rays and diagnostic tests Americans can have? Is it free when American senior citizens, above the age of 70 years, will automatically be deemed, not by a doctor, but by a panel of <u>un-elected government bureaucrats</u>, to be too old to qualify for lifesaving medical services? Instead, *Obamacare* will automatically provide *comfort care* to those Americans who have honorably contributed to America their entire lives? Possibly the most degrading and humiliating feature of *Obamacare* is that Americans will be vulnerable to the whims and wishes of government bureaucrats and potentially cut off from a relationship with a physician whom they have known and trusted for years. What is free about that?

It is encouraging to learn, however, that the prospect of repealing this law is gradually becoming a possibility. The hope is that a decision as to the constitutionality of *Obamacare* will be rendered by the U.S. Supreme Court by the end of June, 2012. However, in spite of this turn of events, the facts remain unchanged. President Barack Obama, Senator Harry Reid, and Congresswoman Nancy Pelosi should be held accountable for their abusive use of power. It was an act of unmitigated arrogance and cunning betrayal for them to have legislatively paved the way in the Congress for the back-door passage of *Obamacare*, which forced upon their fellow-American citizens the indignities of socialized medicine.

Is this really freedom?

What do *you* think?

CHAPTER NINE

The Tea Party Movement

"To compel a man to subsidize with his taxes the propagation of ideas to which he disbelieves and abhors is sinful and tyrannical."
-Thomas Jefferson

Americans have been an accepting and tolerant society; conducting their lives in relative peace and in some semblance of harmony, while placing their trust in their government to responsibly administer the *laws of the land.* However, Americans are paying the price now for their complacency and taking their precious country for granted. Americans are funny, though. They can be pushed; they can probably be pushed again; maybe they can be pushed just a little more one more time. Then watch out. It must be understood that Americans, from all walks of life, will non-violently stand up in the name of freedom and democracy every time, as initially evidenced by the birth of the Tea Party Movement. The early astonishing overthrow of power in:

- Massachusetts, with the election of Republican Scott Brown as U.S. Senator in 2010;
- New Jersey, with the election of Republican Chris Christie as Governor in 2009;
- and Virginia, with the election of Republican Bob McDonnell as Governor, also in 2009,

further illustrates the changing political mindset of Americans and their resolve to protect their country from those who strive to politically control and dominate their lives.

As President Adams explained in an earlier letter again to President Jefferson on August 24, 1815, the Revolutionary War was, *"no part of the revolution; it was only an effect and consequence of it. The (real) revolution was in the minds of the people, and this was effected from 1760-1775, in the course of fifteen years, before a drop of blood was shed at Lexington."*

Mirrored in principle and born of those angry Revolutionary minds that President Adams once described, the Boston Tea Party of 1773 and the Tea Party Movement of today have become similar vehicles by which angry citizens can convene to protest against the audacity of a government that no longer serves as their instrument of freedom. As history tells us, the Boston Tea Party was the result of the increasing anger and resentment spat at Britain after they passed the Tea Act. This Act was a law that forced the colonists to buy tea exclusively from the East India Company, a large global trading corporation of the time, whose many shareholders included Britain. The British lowered the price of the East India Company tea so severely that other more expensive teas available at the time could not compete. They were unjustly taxed, as well. The colonists, boxed in and being threatened not to buy or use other teas, had no choice but to purchase the least expensive tea from the East India Company. The British Parliament voted on this unfair tax behind closed doors, thousands of miles away, and subsequently crammed it down the throats of the colonists. To this day, the concept remains the same. That is, raise taxes on people who already can't afford to pay them; then legislatively bully them into purchasing things they do not want or need. Does health care legislation come to mind?

How about, *bailout?* At the time of the Boston Tea Party, the East India Company was struggling financially, due to massive military debts, and the British wanted to rescue it and restore it to a stronger foundation. The Tea Act was basically designed to undercut the business of the local colonial merchants by British agents selling the tea directly. It was proposed also as a way to ensure that the East India Company would stay in business and that its monopoly on the tea trade in the British Colonies would remain intact. What is the difference between what the British did, in that long ago event, and what President Obama, Harry

Reid and Nancy Pelosi did, on a larger scale, to bail out AIG, Freddie Mac, Fannie Mae, Chrysler, General Motors and the countless banks that should have rescued themselves? Perhaps the East India Company of the past, like the businesses rescued by the Obama Administration of today, was also considered to be *too big to fail.*

"We must not confuse dissent with disloyalty. When the loyal opposition dies, I think the soul of America dies with it."
-Edward R. Murrow, 1954,
Host of "See It Now," reporting on the
Senator Joseph McCarthy-Army hearings
in Washington, DC.

The modern-day Tea Party Movement provides its members with a conservative, organized voice to protest. President Obama does not like it that they are now being heard and have evolved into an effective conservative political movement. At its core, the Tea Party Movement is based on:

- the preservation of America's revered Founding principles;
- lower taxes;
- a return to a smaller, more states-centered government;
- strong fiscally-conservative spending policies;
- and respect for the U.S. Constitution as the hallowed Founding document of this country.

Without question, their intentions are patriotic and honorable. Hopefully, the Tea Party will come to realize that their somewhat inflexible, ultra-conservative, well-intentioned cause could easily become conservatively divisive; thus, potentially helping to hand Barack Obama his re-election in 2012. Those who wish to defeat him have been served, on a shining silver platter, Barack Obama's presidential record that has nothing on it. It is empty and devoid of any positive, helpful programs, policies, and achievements that he could have developed during his presidency. His lack of dedication to the American people speaks just as loudly as his empty rhetoric and patronizing attitude ever could. He has no record of honorably serving the American people. Nothing. Yet, he will run for re-election.

The Tea Party must work to expose him as the man who has almost single-handedly destroyed this great nation; the President who has arrogantly by-passed and disrespected the United States Congress at every turn along the way. The repeated use of his *When-All-Congressional-Means-Fail-Invoke-Executive-Orders*, and the jobs-killing rules and regulations that he persistently continues to impose on American businesses, have served to seriously stifle the American economy; an economy of what should be (and can be again) the most industrious and prosperous nation in the world. The time for UNITY of purpose is now – not after Barack Obama has been re-elected for another four, long, grueling years of his continued quest for power and assault on our freedom.

Is this really freedom?

What do _you_ think?

CHAPTER TEN

The Crisis and Control Factory - Owned and Operated by the Obama Administration

"If you have ten thousand regulations, you destroy all respect for the law."

-Winston Churchill

We are close to losing many of our God-given unalienable rights because of the radical actions and policies of President Obama. He represents all that is self-serving about a misguided, naïve young man, who needs to take serious action to return America to the Founding prominence and stature in the world that it once held and that it has always deserved. It is disheartening to realize, however, that it will never happen, since Barack Obama has been committed to serving only those who seek to fundamentally, piece by piece, law by law, policy by policy tear down that which is the genius of American freedom.

First the Obama Administration manufactures a *crisis*, such as the health care crisis, or the housing crisis, or the financial crisis, which is designed to eventually result in the dependence of Americans on the government. Miraculously, after President Obama deems that Americans have reached the appropriate level of despair, he sweeps in to *repair*, as only he is capable of doing, the problems of the beleaguered citizens of his kingdom. The only solution he has ever had to offer, in his entire tenure in Office, is to raise taxes on the very Americans, who have been financially injured and drained, by his lack of leadership and by his jobs-killing policies, laws, regulations, bailouts and stimulus packages. How can Americans be asked to sustain the onslaught of President Obama's reckless march to socialism and higher taxes, when 12.8 million Americans are out of work *(U.S. Bureau of Labor Statistics, May, 2012)*? That is like putting a person in debtors' prison because he is unable to repay his debts. At that point, President Obama would be most pleased to offer his readily-available government assistance. The circle would be completed. His work would be done.

"We've been a little bit lazy, I think, over the last couple of decades. We've kind of taken for granted – well, people will want to come here (America) and we aren't out there hungry, selling America and trying to attract new business into America," said President Obama, at the Asian Pacific Economic Cooperation (APEC) Conference (November, 2011), which he hosted in Hawaii. Did he accurately portray the United States? President Obama, in short, has done everything possible to tamper with and manipulate America's economy, in order to eventually bring it into a worldwide one-size-fits-all economy. He has imposed many restrictive laws and regulations upon American businesses that have stifled any type of creative entrepreneurship, or the possible expansion and new hiring for existing businesses. The implementation of these regulations continues to feed the hovering economic uncertainty that prohibits businesses from making future business plans. Audaciously, President Obama proclaimed to the world stage that Americans are lazy and are not doing enough to attract new businesses into America. All of this was told to the world by The President of the United States of America, the very person who has diligently worked to help create this fiasco in the first place. Enough!

Is this really freedom?

What do _you_ think?

CHAPTER ELEVEN

The Intruder

"Nearly all men can stand adversity, but if you want to test a man's character, give him power."

-Abraham Lincoln

It is one thing to lead a free people by the equal application of justice and the law for everyone, even making a few mistakes along the way. It is quite another to lead by the aphrodisiac of power alone. Unchecked power, and the arrogance that it spawns, can lead to the invasion of the most sacred essence of mankind; that spirit which shelters the dignity of every person alive. Human dignity, as fragile and vulnerable to the outside transgressions of others as it is, is one of the true paths to every man's soul. No man, not even the President, has the right to diminish the value of another person's life by deeming it insignificant and ordinary. No man, not even the President, has the right to intentionally extinguish the hopes and dreams of our families and friends. By dishonorably using the power of his office, President Obama is economically and socially starving the inspiration that is the foundation of every American's vision for his or her life.

President Obama is under the impression that possessing power excuses him from his duties to equitably apply it towards helping to improve the quality of life and well-being of all Americans. He continues to use and abuse his power to spread his socialist agenda throughout America. He then preaches to the masses, from his pulpit on high, that he is the only one who really knows what Americans *need*. What President Obama does not understand is that his intrusion upon our lives is deeply resented and profoundly unwelcome.

Who in the world is this man? Who in the world does he

think he is? Certainly Barack Obama is not a man of peace; nor is he a man of integrity; nor is he a man who proudly represents all that is truly extraordinary about America and its history of personal courage and sacrifice. He is not, as Thomas Jefferson hoped that he himself would be remembered, *"an honest advocate of my country's rights."* It is clear that President Obama's presidency has been a display of disappointment and disrespect of the American way. It is time for Americans to come together, to non-violently rescue our great nation from his efforts to mastermind its descent into obscurity.

Otherwise, Barack Obama will win. He will have snatched four more years as President to further disable the American economy and bring it into a Third World European forum. The historic downgrade of America's credit rating to a *AA*+, by Standard & Poor's in August, 2011, was largely due to President Obama's arrogant, massive government over-spending. Worse yet is his refusal to seriously consider cutting spending as a first step in solving this very grim and serious problem. The President's signature solution has always been to raise taxes on Americans in our already injured and fragile economy; an economy that is teetering on the brink of yet another recession. Do we really want to endure another four years of President Obama's not-so-disguised mission to intrude upon our lives and take that which is not his?

Is this really freedom?

What do _you_ think?

CHAPTER TWELVE

The Warnings of Two American Presidents

"It is the manners and spirit of a people which preserve a republic in vigor. A degeneracy in these is a canker which soon eats to the heart of its laws and constitution."

-Thomas Jefferson
Notes on the State of Virginia, 1781

James Madison

In a sterling observation, President James Madison (1809-1817) pointed out: *"There are more instances of the abridgement of the freedom of the people by the gradual and silent encroachment of those in power, than by violent and sudden usurpation (conflict)."*

Americans have recently learned some hard and painful lessons; not the least of which is that it is imperative that we continue to be aware of what is happening in the world around us. The *silent encroachment of power*, to which President Madison referred, can still be halted by the informed voices of the American people and by their steadfast protection of and respect for the Constitution of the United States of America. After all, the Constitution is the very soul of American freedom that President Obama took an oath, *"to preserve, protect and defend."* It is clear that knowledge, respect for others, and faith in God, are the greatest deterrents against oppression. An American society, fueled by integrity, that is enlightened and well-informed, will always prevail over and frustrate those who seek to slither their way to power by dishonorable and unscrupulous means.

Ronald Reagan

Another president, Ronald Reagan, in a chilling and eloquent reminder, once cautioned that it is the duty of every American

67

to protect the freedom and liberties that they have inherited through generations of war and sacrifice when he said:

"Freedom is never more than one generation away from extinction. We didn't pass it on to our children in the bloodstream. It must be fought for, protected, and handed on for them to do the same, or one day we will spend our sunset years telling our children and our children's children what it was once like in the United States when men were free."

If we do not wake up now and take serious steps to protect America from the assault on its Founding Principles by President Obama, America will all too quickly reach the day that President Reagan once dreaded. Then its glorious history of individual liberty, filled with promise, opportunity and freedom, could be reduced to the less-than-noteworthy-status of a few pages in a history book, written by a government state robot. Future generations will never know the honor and privilege it is to live in a country that encourages the adventure of personal achievement; nor will they ever experience the exhilarating rush of pride that comes from its success. Barack Obama will have simply robbed them.

America is still, however, the greatest nation on Earth, even with all of its problems, blemishes and controversies. Still, the Obama Administration is stealing freedoms from Americans every day, by forcing their endless restrictions, regulations and unreasonable taxation upon us. Beware then, that their ultimate, true goal is to demean the American spirit to create and excel, so as to aimlessly herd us right down into the pit of mediocrity forever; for ignorance is always intimidated by the skill and achievement of others.

Is this really freedom?

What do *you* think?

CHAPTER THIRTEEN

President Barack Obama and the Aftermath of His Presidency

"Fellow citizens, we cannot escape history. We…will be remembered in spite of ourselves. No personal significance of insignificance can spare one or another of us. The fiery trial through which we pass will light us down in honor or dishonor, to the latest generation."
-Abraham Lincoln

The title of President of the United States of America conveys prestige, honor and integrity. The enormous power and authority granted to the President must be tempered with courage, humility, discipline and trust. A great president will then use that power wisely to protect the Constitution and foster a thriving America that is based on the success and well-being of the individual citizen.

No president will likely serve without a few *blunders* for the record books. Some presidents will forever live prominently in history, because of the merits of their accomplishments while in office. Others will leave quieter legacies. Regardless, a president should leave a legacy worthy of respect; a legacy that reflects the efforts of a President's administration to honorably serve and protect the American people. However, President Obama is actively building an expanding list of his dishonorable use of power. He will be remembered for his radical actions and policies when it comes to Illegal Immigration, Terrorism, the Mosque at Ground Zero, his failure to enforce the American Rule of Law, his intentional disabling of the American economy, *Obamacare,* and more. It is unfortunate that his policies have been based solely on the political ramifications each will have for his 2012 re-election campaign. Perhaps in the long-run of history, President Barack Obama will be remembered for the contempt he has shown for the Americans he was supposed to serve and the Constitution he was supposed to protect.

Is this really freedom?

What do _you_ think?

CHAPTER FOURTEEN

Americans Must Use Their Magnificent Power to Vote!

"Elections belong to the people. It is their decision. If they decide to turn their backs on the fire and burn their behinds, then they will just have to sit on their blisters."

-Abraham Lincoln

What happened then is happening now. The similarities of the irrevocable damage that results from government oppression and the descent of a free country into socialism remain unchanged today. In 1850, Frederic Bastiat, a French economist, statesman and author, eloquently wrote of liberty in his pamphlet entitled, *The Law,* that we have been given by God all that we need, in order to define our individual destinies of personal autonomy. He warned that the interference of the government and its yearning for a society based on the insignificance of the individual will surely lead to the fall of freedom. He wrote:

> *"God has given to men all that is necessary for them to accomplish their destinies. He has provided a social form, as well as a human form. And these social organs of persons are so constituted that they will develop themselves harmoniously in the clean air of liberty.*
> * *Away then, with quacks and organizers!*
> * *Away with their rings, chains, hooks and pincers!*
> * *Away with their artificial systems!*
> * *Away with the whims of governmental administrators,*
> * *their socialized projects, their centralization,*
> * *their tariffs, their government schools, their state religions,*

- *their free credit, their bank monopolies, their regulations,*
- *their restrictions, their equalization by taxation and their pious moralizations!*

And now that the legislators and do-gooders have so futilely inflicted so many systems upon society, may they finally end where they should have begun: May they reject all systems, and try liberty; for liberty is an acknowledgement of faith in God and His works."

-Frederic Bastiat,
"The Law," 1850

In spite of President Obama's undisguised quest for power, it is the American citizens who hold the ultimate, supreme power to change and eliminate the injustices to which Mr. Bastiat referred in *The Law.* We have our magnificent power to vote.

Americans must use their power in a massive turnout to vote in the November, 2012 Presidential Election. This election will determine, possibly forever, the destiny of American freedom and the relevance of the hallowed Constitution of the United States of America. This is not a game. It is very real. It's time for Americans to come alive; to unite and work to protect their country. We can do it! We have the magnificent power to vote. We must use it!

> *"Let each citizen remember at the moment*
> *he is offering his vote that he is not making*
> *a present or a compliment to please*
> *an individual -- or at least that he ought*
> *not so to do; but he is executing*
> *the most solemn trust in human society*
> *for which he is accountable*
> *to God and his country."*
>
> *--Samuel Adams,*
> *American Revolutionary Patriot and*
> *Signer of The Declaration of Independence*

Now *this* is freedom!

What do *you* think?

CAROL POLZIN

CONCLUSION

"All tyranny needs to gain a foothold is for people of good conscience to remain silent."

-Thomas Jefferson

Speak up!

If we believe what President Obama is telling us; that we are incapable of handling our own lives without his interference, then we have become the problem, not the solution. We are decent, honorable Americans who have made millions of vital, significant contributions to the world in the name of freedom and improving the human condition. The significance of these contributions far outweigh the efforts of President Obama to restructure and take over our lives. Where is our honor? Why do we let him get away with it? Are our heads buried so deeply in the sand that we cannot see, or we pretend not to see, the damage that his disregard for this country has brought upon us?

Or, is it just easier to let someone else tell us how and what to think? If so, our priorities must change. America must come first. The Obama Administration is counting on our uncharacteristic passivity and complacency. We are a proud, generous, compassionate people. What has happened to us? We have become so very self-absorbed and have ignored the ever-increasing attempts of this administration to take away the self-reliance that was born from our American entrepreneurial spirit. This provides a wide open door for them to peddle their wares of big government power and control to an unsuspecting and preoccupied nation. Hopefully, we now recognize that President Obama's friendly and charming façade masks the ulterior motives of a man who came to compromise the sovereignty of the most magnificent nation on Earth. So we

75

must reclaim our moral courage. Who are we not to protect the freedom that has been passed on to us through the Ages? It is our duty to do so. Our country needs us.

Americans feel angry, helpless, frustrated and confused. We must turn this negative energy into a united, positive force to rescue America from the clutches of socialism and the decay of American freedom and our rights that will surely result. This is our last chance to do so. In voting booths all across America, a patriotic unity of purpose could bring about stunning results. We can do it. We're Americans!

We all must speak up before President Obama succeeds in wiping out the free and democratic American way of life that we cherish so much today. For it is clear that history will never forgive an America that was destroyed by the ambivalence of its own citizens towards the efforts of President Barack Obama to silence the rhapsody of their freedom. Should that ever be the case, then let it be known: Americans will deserve everything they get.

Freedom's calling! Will you answer?

IT'S UP TO US NOW!

Some Ways to Contribute Your Time and Talents:

- Register to vote
- Remind friends and family to register to vote.
- Place campaign signs on your lawn.
- Hand out campaign flyers door-to-door.
- Make a financial contribution to your candidate's campaign.
- Call your local radio talk show stations and voice your opinion.
- Write Letters to the Editor.
- March in local parades to support your candidate.
- Serve as an Election Judge at your local precinct polling place on Election Day, November 6, 2012.
    - o Call or visit your Secretary of State's Office website for specific details of Election Judges' duties and qualifications.
    - o Connect with your local County Auditor's Office to apply to be an Election Judge.
- Volunteer at your state/local political campaign office:
    - o Assist with mailings.
    - o Help with data entry.
    - o Update files
    - o Answer phones
    - o Make phone calls in support of your candidate.
- VOTE on Tuesday, November 6, 2012!

CAROL POLZIN

"The world is a dangerous place to live, not because of the people who are evil, but because of the people who don't do anything about it."

-Albert Einstein

For more information or to contact Carol,
please visit:

FreedomsCalling.com

www.ingramcontent.com/pod-product-compliance
Lightning Source LLC
Chambersburg PA
CBHW021234280526

45784CB00005B/2094